Article 7

The Right to Birth Registration,
Name and Nationality, and the Right to Know
and Be Cared for by Parents

A Commentary on the United Nations Convention
on the Rights of the Child

Editors

André Alen, Johan Vande Lanotte, Eugeen Verhellen,
Fiona Ang, Eva Berghmans and Mieke Verheyde

Article 7

The Right to Birth Registration, Name and Nationality, and the Right to Know and Be Cared for by Parents

Ineta Ziemele
Riga Graduate School of Law

MARTINUS
NIJHOFF
PUBLISHERS

LEIDEN • BOSTON
2007

This book is printed on acid-free paper.

A Cataloging-in-Publication record for this book is available from the Library of Congress.

Cite as: I. Ziemele, "Article 7: The Right to Birth Registration, Name and Nationality, and the Right to Know and Be Cared for by Parents", in: A. Alen, J. Vande Lanotte, E. Verhellen, F. Ang, E. Berghmans and M. Verheyde (Eds.) *A Commentary on the United Nations Convention on the Rights of the Child* (Martinus Nijhoff Publishers, Leiden, 2007).

ISSN 1574-8626
ISBN 978-90-04-14863-5

© 2007 by Koninklijke Brill NV, Leiden, The Netherlands.
Koninklijke Brill NV incorporates the imprints Brill, Hotei Publishers,
IDC Publishers, Martinus Nijhoff Publishers and VSP.

Cover image by Nadia, 1 1/2 years old

http://www.brill.nl

PRINTED IN THE NETHERLANDS

CONTENTS

List of Abbreviations vii
Author Biography ix
Text of Article 7 xi

Chapter One. Introduction 1
Chapter Two. Comparison with Related International
  Human Rights Provisions 3
  1. Survey of Related International and Regional Instruments 3
  2. Analysis of the Related International and Regional Provisions 7
    2.1 The Right to Registration Immediately After the Birth
      and the Right to a Name 8
    2.2 The Right of a Child to a Nationality and the Prohibition
      of Statelessness 12
    2.3 Non-Discrimination Rule 16
Chapter Three. Scope of Article 7 21
  1. '[C]hild Shall Be Registered Immediately After Birth' 21
  2. '[T]he Right From Birth to a Name' 23
  3. '[T]he Right to Acquire a Nationality' 23
  4. '[T]he Right to Know and Be Cared for by His or Her Parents' 26
  5. '[I]n Accordance with Their National Law . . . and . . . Relevant
    International Instruments' 28
  6. '[I]n Particular Where the Child Would Otherwise Be Stateless' 28
Chapter Four. Conclusions 31

LIST OF ABBREVIATIONS

ACHPR	African Charter on Human and Peoples' Rights 1981
ACHR	American Convention on Human Rights 1969
CCPR	International Covenant on Civil and Political Rights 1966
CERD	International Convention on the Elimination of All Forms of Racial Discrimination 1965
CERD Committee	Committee on the Elimination of Racial Discrimination
CRC	International Convention on the Rights of the Child 1989
CRC Committee	UN Committee on the Rights of the Child
ECN	European Convention on Nationality 1997
ICJ	International Court of Justice
ILC	International Law Commission
UDHR	Universal Declaration of Human Rights 1948
UN	United Nations

AUTHOR BIOGRAPHY

Ineta Ziemele holds a law degree (University of Latvia), as well as the degree of Master of International Law (Raoul Wallenberg Institute and University of Lund, Sweden) and Doctor of Law (University of Cambridge, United Kingdom). From 1992 to 1995, she worked as adviser to the Foreign Affairs Committee of the Parliament of Latvia and in 1995 as adviser to the Prime Minister. She was a founding director of the Institute on Human Rights at the Faculty of Law of the University of Latvia (1995–99), where she also lectured in International and European Law. From 1999 to 2001 she was a Programme Adviser at the Directorate General of Human Rights, Council of Europe. She founded and was editor-in-chief of the Baltic Yearbook of International Law. Until 2005, she held the positions of Söderberg Professor of International Law and Human Rights (Riga Graduate School of Law, Latvia) and of visiting Professor at the Raoul Wallenberg Institute (Faculty of Law, Lund University, Sweden). On 27 April 2005, she was appointed Judge of the European Court of Human Rights.

TEXT OF ARTICLE 7

ARTICLE 7

1. The child shall be registered immediately after birth and shall have the right from birth to a name, the right to acquire a nationality and, as far as possible, the right to know and be cared for by his or her parents.

2. States Parties shall ensure the implementation of these rights in accordance with their national law and their obligations under the relevant international instruments in this field, in particular where the child would otherwise be stateless.

ARTICLE 7

1. L'enfant est enregistré aussitôt sa naissance et a dès celle-ci le droit à un nom, le droit d'acquérir une nationalité et, dans la mesure du possible, le droit de connaître ses parents et d'être élevé par eux.

2. Les Etats parties veillent à mettre ces droits en œuvre conformément à leur législation nationale et aux obligations que leur imposent les instruments internationaux applicables en la matière, en particulier dans les cas où faute de cela l'enfant se trouverait apatride.

CHAPTER ONE

INTRODUCTION*

1. The UN Committee on the Rights of the Child (CRC Committee) in its General Comment No. 7 on Implementing Child Rights in Early Childhood recognized that the UN Convention on the Rights of the Child (CRC) requires that children, including the very youngest children, be respected as persons in their own right.[1] The Committee further stated: "Comprehensive services for early childhood begin at birth. The Committee notes that provision for registration of all children at birth is still a major challenge for many countries and regions. This can impact negatively on a child's sense of personal identity and children may be denied entitlements to basic health, education and social welfare. As a first step in ensuring the rights to survival, development and access to quality services for all children (Art. 6), the Committee recommends that States Parties take all necessary measures to ensure that all children are registered at birth."[2] Even if the CRC Committee in its Comment does not mention specifically Article 7, it is there that the CRC provides for the right to registration at birth. The Comment draws extensively on the primary role of parents in promoting children's development and well-being, although it does not refer specifically to Article 7 and the right to know and be cared for by parents provided therein. It is equally interesting to note that the rights to a name and nationality also contained in this Article do not form part of the measures that the CRC Committee underlines as essential for the purposes of implementing child rights in early childhood.

2. The above approach of the CRC Committee raises questions as concerns the scope of Article 7 of the CRC. There is no general comment which addresses specifically issues of registration and nationality and thus provides guidelines on the scope of the Article. It is therefore proposed to comment on Article 7 taking into consideration relevant international and

---

* December 2004, updated in September 2006.
[1] CRC Committee, *General Comment No. 7. Implementing Child Rights in Early Childhood* (UN Doc. CRC/C/GC/7, 2005), para. 5.
[2] *Ibid.*, para. 25.

regional human rights instruments and the available State practice as well as the decisions of international tribunals with regard to issues of registration, name and nationality. It has to be pointed out that the regulation of nationality has long been on the agenda of the development of international law and that some of the achievements and problems are equally relevant when looking specifically at the right to a nationality of a child.[3] The structure of the commentary follows this approach. Chapter Two lists relevant provisions in other international and regional instruments and provides an analysis of these provisions in the attempt to decipher the minimum international standard as concerns the registration of a child after the birth, the right to a name, the right to a nationality and a corollary obligation of prohibition of statelessness. It also outlines the non-discrimination rule since there is a general agreement and it has also been emphasised by the CRC Committee that discrimination renders the enjoyment of rights meaningless. Chapter Three comments on all the rights contained in Article 7 separately, taking into consideration the conclusions arrived at in the previous chapter. The scope of the Article is also determined by reference to general observations of the CRC Committee in relation to specific country situations since this represents a useful source of State practice as well as its assessment against the applicable law. Finally, the commentary offers some conclusions.

---

[3] For the historical perspective see among others R. Donner, *The Regulation of Nationality in International Law* (2nd ed., Irvington-on-Hudson, Transnational Publishers, 1994); I. Ziemele, *State Continuity and Nationality: the Baltic States and Russia. Past, Present and Future as Defined by International Law* (Leiden/Boston, Martinus Nijhoff Publishers, 2005), chapters 9 and 12.

CHAPTER TWO

COMPARISON WITH RELATED INTERNATIONAL
HUMAN RIGHTS PROVISIONS

1. *Survey of Related International and Regional Instruments*

3. The 1966 International Covenant on Civil and Political Rights (CCPR)[4] provides in Article 24 that:

> '1. Every child shall have, without any discrimination as to race, colour, sex, language, religion, national or social origin, property or birth, the right to such measures of protection as are required by his status as a minor, on the part of his family, society and the State.
> 2. Every child shall be registered immediately after birth and shall have a name.
> 3. Every child has the right to acquire a nationality.'

4. Related provisions are to be found in the 1948 Universal Declaration of Human Rights (UDHR)[5] which provides for the general right to a nationality in Article 15. The 1965 International Convention on the Elimination of All Forms of Racial Discrimination (CERD)[6] in Article 1 determines racial discrimination. Article 5 provides for an extensive list of human rights and freedoms, including the right to a nationality, whose effective enjoyment has to be guaranteed to everyone without discrimination on the basis of race, ethnic or national origin. Although the Committee on the Elimination of Racial Discrimination (CERD Committee) does not have a specific mandate to address instances of discrimination of children on the basis of race, ethnic or national origin, it is not precluded from noting them whenever problems arise in the wider context of its mandate.[7]

---

[4] United Nations, International Covenant on Civil and Political Rights, adopted on 16 December 1966, entered into force on 23 March 1976, http://www.ohchr.org/english/law/ccpr.htm.

[5] United Nations, Universal Declaration on Human Rights, adopted on 10 December 1948, http://www.unhchr.ch/udhr/lang/eng.htm.

[6] United Nations, International Convention on the Elimination of All Forms of Racial Discrimination, adopted on 21 December 1965, entered into force on 4 January 1969, http://www.ohchr.org/english/law/cerd.htm.

[7] CERD Committee, *Concluding Observations: Latvia* (UN Doc. CERD/C/304/Add. 79, 1999), para. 12. The CERD Committee notes that non-Latvian ethnic groups are in a discriminatory position since they have to apply for citizenship. Even if the procedure has been made more accessible for elderly persons and for children, the process remains slow.

5. The 1969 American Convention on Human Rights (ACHR)[8] in Article 19 deals with the rights of the child. It provides that:

> 'Every minor child has the right to the measures of protection required by his condition as a minor on the part of his family, society, and the State.'

Article 20 deals with the right to nationality recognizing that every person has the right to a nationality. For the purposes of the discussion on Article 7 of the CRC, the following part of this Article is of relevance. It states:

> '2. Every person has the right to the nationality of the state in whose territory he was born if he does not have the right to any other nationality.'

6. The 1981 African Charter on Human and Peoples' Rights (ACHPR)[9] does not contain the rights to registration or nationality. In Article 18(3), the Charter provides that:

> '3. The State shall ensure the elimination of every discrimination against women and also ensure the protection of the rights of the woman and the child as stipulated in international declarations and conventions.'

7. For the purposes of the Charter, the CRC is the minimum standard which would include Article 7. This was clearly an insufficient approach which prompted the adoption of the 1990 African Charter on the Rights and Welfare of the Child.[10] In Article 6, entitled 'Name and nationality', the minimum international standard concerning the legal status of children is spelled out. The Article provides:

> '1. Every child shall have the right from his birth to a name.
> 2. Every child shall be registered immediately after birth.
> 3. Every child has the right to acquire a nationality.
> 4. States Parties to the present Charter shall undertake to ensure that their Constitutional legislation recognize the principles according to which a child shall acquire the nationality of the State in the territory of which he has been born if, at the time of the child's birth, he is not granted nationality by any other State in accordance with its laws.'

---

[8] Organization of American States, American Convention on Human Rights, adopted on 22 November 1969, entered into force on 18 July 1978, http://www.oas.org/juridico/english/Treaties/b-32.htm.

[9] African Union, African Charter on Human and Peoples' Rights, adopted on 27 June 1981, entered into force on 21 October 1986, http://www.africa-union.org/official_documents/Treaties_%20Conventions_%20Protocols/Banjul%20Charter.pdf.

[10] African Union, African Charter on the Rights and Welfare of the Child, adopted on 11 July 1990, entered into force on 29 November 1999, http://www.africa-union.org/root/au/Documents/Treaties/Text/A.%20C.%20ON%20THE%20RIGHT%20AND%20WELF%20OF%20CHILD.pdf.

8. There are no provisions on the right to a nationality[11] or the rights of children in the European Convention on Human Rights (ECHR).[12] The European Court of Human Rights (ECtHR) has dealt with several issues related to the rights of a child in the framework of Article 8 of the ECHR dealing with the right to family life and privacy.[13]

9. In the Council of Europe framework, the States have adopted the European Convention on the Exercise of Children's Rights.[14] The aim of the Convention is to determine the status and rights of children in different domestic proceedings. Article 1(2) determines the object of the Convention as follows:

> '2. The object of the present Convention is, in the best interests of children, to promote their rights, to grant them procedural rights and to facilitate the exercise of these rights by ensuring that children are, themselves or through other persons or bodies, informed and allowed to participate in proceedings affecting them before a judicial authority.'

10. In 1997, the Council of Europe adopted the European Convention on Nationality (ECN).[15] It states that the right to a nationality and the prohibition of statelessness are the main principles of the Convention (Article 4) and that these principles also apply in situations of territorial changes (Articles 18 to 20). The Convention contains some provisions that are aimed

---

[11] The European Court of Human Rights has repeatedly held that the Convention and its Protocols do not provide for the right to a nationality, although some exceptional cases of arbitrary decisions might fall within the Court's competence either under Articles 6 or 8. See ECtHR, Decision on the admissibility of Application No. 48321/99 by *Tatjana Slivenko and others* v. *Latvia*, 23 January 2002, Reports of Judgments and Decisions 2002–II., paras 77–78; ECtHR, Decision on the admissibility of Application No. 50183/99 by *Aleksandr Kolosovskiy* v. *Latvia*, 29 January 2004, p. 16.

[12] Council of Europe, European Convention for the Protection of Human Rights and Fundamental Freedoms, adopted on 4 November 1950, entered into force on 3 September 1953, http://conventions.coe.int/Treaty/en/Treaties/Html/005.htm.

[13] On child custody, see, *inter alia*, ECtHR, *Margaret and Roger Andersson* v. *Sweden*, 25 February 1992, Reports of Judgments and Decisions 1997–IV. On the right to family life in cases involving an immigrant parent, see ECtHR, *Berrehab* v. *Netherlands*, 21 June 1988, Series A, No 138; ECtHR, *Ciliz* v. *Netherlands*, 11 July 2000, Judgments and Decisions 2000–VIII. On access to files recording children in need of care, see ECtHR, *Gaskin* v. *United Kingdom*, 23 June 1989, Series A, No 160. On language in education and respect for private and family life, see ECtHR, *Case 'relating to certain aspects of the laws on the use of languages in education in Belgium'* v. *Belgium (Belgian Linguistic Case)*, 23 July 1968, Series A, No 6.

[14] Council of Europe, European Convention on the Exercise of Children's Rights, adopted on 25 January 1996, entered into force on 1 July 2000, http://conventions.coe.int/Treaty/en/Treaties/Html/160.htm.

[15] Council of Europe, European Convention on Nationality, adopted on 6 November 1997, entered into force on 1 March 2000, http://conventions.coe.int/Treaty/en/Treaties/Html/166.htm.

at avoiding statelessness among children. Territorial changes, such as State succession, create many uncertainties as to the legal status of individuals affected by such changes. That especially concerns children because in the context of changing governmental and legal structures, their rights to represent their interests are particularly diminished. The determination of the rights and the status of minors thus more then ever depends on the family and the States concerned. In the 1990s, the Council of Europe and the International Law Commission (ILC) carried out an important work in codifying and developing rules on nationality in the context of State succession. The ECN develops general rules that apply also in cases of territorial changes. The ILC Articles on Nationality of Natural Persons in relation to the Succession of States[16] contain an Article on the status of children in such situations. Article 13 states that:

> 'A child of a person concerned, born after the date of the succession of States, who has not acquired any nationality, has the right to the nationality of the State concerned on whose territory that child was born.'

11. In addition to territorial changes, there are other circumstances that may affect children seriously. Notably, it happens when they are forced to leave their own country alone or together with their parents and seek protection in other countries. The 1951 Convention relating to the Status of Refugees[17] and its 1967 Protocol[18] as well as the Convention relating to the Status of Stateless Persons[19] and applicable rules of international humanitarian law will be relevant along with the CRC provisions (Article 22) in ensuring that children have a recognized status in various circumstances and enjoy at least the minimum rights that these international instruments set forth.[20]

---

[16] International Law Commission, Articles on Nationality of Natural Persons in relation to the Succession of States, text adopted by the Commission at its fifty-first session, in 1999, and submitted to the UN General Assembly as part of the Commission's report covering the work of that session, *Official Records of the General Assembly, Fifty-fourth Session, Supplement No. 10 (A/54/10)*, http://untreaty.un.org/ilc/texts/3_4.htm.

[17] United Nations, Convention relating to the Status of Refugees, adopted on 28 July 1951, entered into force on 22 April 1954, http://www.ohchr.org/english/law/refugees.htm.

[18] United Nations, Protocol relating to the Status of Refugees, adopted on 31 January 1967, entered into force on 4 October 1967, http://www.ohchr.org/english/law/protocolrefugees.htm.

[19] United Nations, Convention relating to the Status of Stateless Persons, adopted on 28 September 1954, entered into force on 6 June 1960, http://www.ohchr.org/english/law/stateless.htm.

[20] In detail on the rights provided for by the CRC in situations of unaccompanied and separated children outside their country of origin, see CRC Committee, *General Comment No. 6. Treatment of Unaccompanied and Separated Children Outside Their Country of Origin* (UN Doc. CRC/GC/2005/6, 2005).

12. The EU Charter of Fundamental Rights and Freedoms[21] in Article 24 determines the rights of the child without mentioning specifically the rights related to the legal status of a child in the territory of child's birth or residence. The Article uses a very broad formula, i.e., 'children shall have the right to such protection and care as is necessary for their well-being'. Since in the explanations to the Article it is mentioned that the Article is based, *inter alia*, on the CRC, it can be presumed that the scope of Article 7 is integrated into Article 24 of the EU Charter.[22] The EU Charter does not deal with the issue of nationality. In the Chapter on citizens' rights it refers to the concept of EU citizenship which is defined in the Treaty on European Union. The EU citizenship is built on the national citizenship, as determined and granted by the EU Member States. The added value of the EU Charter is that it requires the EU institutions in their decision-making activities to make sure that the rights of the child are not jeopardized.

2. Analysis of the Related International and Regional Provisions

13. The provisions listed above indicate several key issues that are important in order to ensure the rights of a child. The first issue is the recognition of a child immediately after the birth by the legal order of the State concerned. The main instruments of such recognition are: registration of a child with the name and taking a decision on his/her nationality. The CRC has added the third element, *i.e.* recognition of the child by the parents or, at least, the right of a child to know who the parents are (*cf. infra*, Chapter Three, 4). The following analysis will address the applicable provisions presented above in more detail. The focus of attention will be the following questions. First, the scope and content of the right to registration immediately after the birth. Second, the scope and content of the right of a child to a nationality in general and in situations of State succession. The applicability of the non-discrimination rule will be introduced since Article 24 of the CCPR restates it specifically despite a general provision in Article 2. The analysis will make a particular reference to the CCPR. The findings will subsequently serve as a point of departure for analysis and conclusions on Article 7 of the CRC.

---

[21] European Union, Charter of Fundamental Rights and Freedoms, adopted on 18 December 2000, http://ec.europa.eu/justice_home/unit/charte/index_en.html.
[22] Bureau of the Convention Responsible for Drafting the Charter of Fundamental Rights, *Charter of Fundamental Rights of the European Union. Explanations relating to the complete text of the Charter*, December 2000 (European Union, 2001), p. 41.

2.1   *The Right to Registration Immediately After the Birth and the Right to a Name*

14. In accordance with Article 24(2) of the CCPR, every child must be registered and given a name immediately after birth. The UN Human Rights Committee has emphasised that the duty to register a child is closely linked with the right of a child to special measures of protection and 'it is designed to promote recognition of the child's legal personality'.[23] During the drafting of Article 24, the right to registration was not part of the initial proposal. The proposal contained the right to a name and a nationality. In view of a heated debate on the latter, a new proposal was submitted concerning registration.[24] The drafting history tells that there was a view that the granting of a nationality had to be seen as the best recognition of a child by domestic law. States could not however agree on an international standard in this respect at the time of the drafting of the CCPR. They had to settle for a compromise, *i.e.* the right to register a child after the birth which may not entail the granting of a nationality, on the one hand, and the right to acquire nationality, on the other hand. The two procedures can be different and, in practice, they often are.

15. Neither the Covenant, nor the Human Rights Committee explain what 'immediate' registration means. It is left to States to determine the registration procedure in accordance with their national laws. It is clear, however, that for the purposes of Article 24 the reference to 'immediate' registration implies a much shorter period of time than, for example, references to 'reasonable time' in the context of a fair trial. We are talking days and weeks rather than months and years. This seems to be in line with the fundamental right of a child to special protection. It is clear that if a child is not registered he/she may be prevented from the benefits provided and protection afforded by the State. The Human Rights Committee has commented that the lack of registration may result in discrimination and be seen as contrary to Articles 24, 26 and 27 of the CCPR, if it is directed to a particular ethnic group.[25] At the same time, one can notice that over the years the Committee, similar to other treaty monitoring bodies, has started

---

[23] Human Rights Committee, *General Comment No. 17. Rights of the Child (Article 24), 1989* (reproduced in UN Doc. HRI/GEN/1/Rev.5, 2001), para. 7.
[24] See S. Detrick, *A Commentary on the United Nations Convention on the Rights of the Child* (The Hague/Boston/London, Martinus Nijhoff Publishers, 1999), pp. 144–145.
[25] Human Rights Committee, *Concluding Observations: Syrian Arab Republic* (UN Doc. CCPR/CO/71/SYR, 2001), para. 27.

exercising more pressure on States in the area of the granting of nationality to children, thereby confirming that statelessness is a considerable problem for children, even if they are properly registered (*cf. infra*, Chapter Two, 2.2).[26] In other words, registration of a child does not always ensure his/her rights and discrimination in the enjoyment may arise because of the lack of nationality. This has been acknowledged by treaty monitoring bodies (also *infra*, Chapter Two, 2.3).[27]

16. A related question arises whether, in case of parental negligence or otherwise a child is not being registered with the State, the latter has a positive obligation to seek out the child. In accordance with the information that the Human Rights Committee requires States to provide in their reports in this respect, one could read a certain positive obligation to ensure registration of a child after his/her birth. The Committee explains that such an obligation on the part of the State is aimed at reducing 'the danger of abduction, sale of or traffic in children'.[28] In other words, in view of the vulnerability of children and the special protection that they are entitled to as a result, the State not only has the obligation to establish a legal framework that allows for the registration of a child after the birth, but it also has to actively ensure that children are registered, since this helps to provide their security and guarantees the enjoyment of other rights.[29]

17. For example, the obligations that the Council of Europe Member States have under the European Convention on the Exercise of Children's Rights can only be ensured when and if the States concerned have the functioning system of registration of children after the birth. The European Convention details the procedural rights of children in the so-called family proceedings in front of the judiciary.

---

[26] The Human Rights Committee recommends that 'the State Party should take urgent steps to find a solution to the statelessness of numerous Kurds in Syria and to allow Kurdish children born in Syria to acquire Syrian nationality'. Human Rights Committee, *Concluding Observations: Syrian Arab Republic* (UN Doc. CCPR/CO/71/SYR, 2001), para. 27.

[27] See *e.g.* CERD Committee, *General Recommendation No. 30: Discrimination Against Non Citizens*, (CERD Gen.Rec.No. 30, 2004), para. 16. The recommendation invites States to reduce statelessness, in particular among children. The Committee considers that 'under the Convention, differential treatment based on citizenship or immigration status will constitute discrimination if the criteria for such differentiation, judged in the light of the objectives and purposes of the Convention, are not applied pursuant to a legitimate aim, and are not proportional to the achievement of this aim.'

[28] Human Rights Committee, *o.c.* (note 23), para. 7.

[29] Further on this point, *cf. infra*, Chapter Three, 1 (note 66).

18. The Human Rights Committee has had the possibility to address some aspects of the application of the CCPR in situations where the family resides on the territory of the State Party unlawfully. It is obvious that in situations of illegal immigrants children are particularly vulnerable to abuse. In the case of Winata and Lan Li against Australia, lodged by an Indonesian family residing unlawfully for many years in Australia, the Human Rights Committee took an opinion that the family should not be extradited to Indonesia because that would violate the rights of their child in accordance with Article 24 and the right to a family.[30] A child was born in Australia, was a citizen and had never known any other country. Even if Australia had good grounds to expel the parents because they had violated the Australian immigration legislation, the interests and rights of the child to a family were given more weight by the Human Rights Committee.

19. It has been repeatedly recognized that children are particularly vulnerable when they flee their own country alone or together with parents and are subject to procedures determining whether they are entitled to asylum and a refugee status. This is, of course, a different question from registration of a child at birth and a decision on nationality at the time. It is, nevertheless, important to see that in the country there may be children with different legal status. The question of the respect of their rights without discrimination based on their status may arise (*cf. infra*, Chapter Two, 2.3).

20. It has been argued that Article 7 of the CRC is closely linked to Article 8 on the right of a child to identity. Name and nationality are seen as elements of identity. Article 24(2) of the CCPR contains the right to a name. The European Court of Human Rights has dealt with the issue of the right to a name in the framework of Article 8 of the ECHR, considering it part of the right to privacy. The Court has left a rather wide margin of appreciation to States in relation to many aspects of the recognition of personal names within their legal systems.[31] It derives from the Court's case law that Article 8 might be violated in the area of personal names if the State has not avoided situations in which the personal name of a child may have acquired an offensive meaning through the process of recognition and/or

---

[30] Human Rights Committee, *Winata and Lan Li v. Australia, Communication No. 930/2000* (UN Doc. CCPR/C/72/D/930/2000, 2001), paras. 7(2) and 7(3).

[31] ECtHR, *Burghartz* v. *Switzerland*, 22 February 1994, Series A280–B; ECtHR, *Stjerna* v. *Finland*, 25 November 1994, Series A299–B; ECtHR, *Guillot* v. *France*, 24 October 1996, Reports 1996–V.

transliteration, where necessary, in domestic legal frameworks. Secondly, the regulation of attribution of personal names by the State could indeed be excessive and create considerable practical difficulties to individuals. In other words, the State might use its margin of appreciation disproportionally. The Court will intervene in such cases if brought to its attention.

21. Registration of a child, *i.e.* recognition by a legal system concerned, requires that a child is given a name. As exemplified, the State has a certain obligation to limit the parental freedom in their choice of the name in case the name is contrary to the best interests of the child. The CERD Committee has noted further that 'the name of an individual is a fundamental aspect of the culture and ethnic identity' and in this respect the State is under an obligation to respect the particularities of children belonging to ethnic groups.[32] In other words, the right to a name is not simply an attribute of the registration of a child. It is an autonomous right that is closely linked to the identity and culture of the person concerned and, as such, it is protected in relevant human rights instruments giving rise to specific obligations on the part of States. The difference seems to arise in the degree of margin of appreciation left to States in regulating the spelling and writing of names in accordance with the traditions and possible specific characteristics of the official languages. Different treaty monitoring bodies, depending on their mandate, may have varying possibilities to influence these choices.[33]

---

[32] CERD Committee, *Concluding Observations: Japan* (UN Doc. CERD/C/304/Add.114, 2001), para. 18. Also Article 11 of the Council of Europe Framework Convention for the Protection of National Minorities states that:

> '1. The Parties undertake to recognise that every person belonging to a national minority has the right to use his or her surname (patronym) and first names in the minority language and the right to official recognition of them, according to modalities provided for in their legal system.'

[33] It was noted that the European Court of Human Rights has so far been leaving a wide margin of appreciation for States in this area. From the point of view of minority rights, especially if the need for special measures is considered, the margin may be narrower in relation to persons belonging to a minority. As for the Court's case law, this question is still open. See ECtHR, Decision on the admissibility of application No. 715570/01 by *Kuharec v. Latvia*, 7 December 2004. Also: Decision on the admissibility of application No. 71074/01 by *Mentzen v. Latvia*, 7 December 2004, Reports of Judgments and Decisions 2004-XII. The difference between these two cases is that only in the *Kuharec* case the applicant brought up the minority rights aspect.

2.2   The Right of a Child to a Nationality and the Prohibition of Statelessness

22. The obligation to register a child is linked to the decision on the nationality of a child. The CCPR does not provide for the general right to a nationality, but Article 24(3) CCPR provides that 'every child has a right to acquire a nationality'. It has to be noted that this is a weaker form of the right as compared to Article 15 of the UDHR providing for the general right to a nationality. Article 15 of the UDHR is not, however, considered to have become part of customary international law.[34] This conforms to the still persisting opposition by States as concerns any developments in international law regulating their competence to determine who their nationals are.[35] States are not, however, considered to have unlimited freedom in their regulation of nationality, as illustrated by Article 1 of the Convention on Certain Questions relating to the Conflict of Nationality Laws, signed in the Hague on 12 April 1930,[36] which provides that:

> 'It is for each State to determine under its own law who are its nationals. This law shall be recognised by other States in so far as it is consistent with international conventions, international custom, and the principles of law generally recognised with regard to nationality.'

23. It has been said that this treaty provision reflects what is currently considered to be the rule of customary international law. The crucial question is then whether, and to what extent, there exist such generally recognised principles of law or accepted provisions of international conventions which impose limitations on the competence of a State to determine nationality in general and in relation to children more specifically.

24. Article 7 of the CRC takes the CCPR approach and the practice of the Human Rights Committee thus can be very instructive. It is generally accepted that individuals are nationals upon their birth through *jus sanguinis* or *jus soli* principles, or a combination of both, depending on which approach the

---

[34] I. Ziemele and G. Schram, 'Article 15', in: G. Alfredsson and A. Eide (eds.), *The Universal Declaration of Human Rights: A Common Standard of Achievement* (The Hague/London/Boston, Martinus Nijhoff Publishers, 1999), pp. 297–323.

[35] Among the writings on nationality in international law, see I. Brownlie, 'The Relations of Nationality in Public International Law', *British Yearbook of International Law*, vol. 39, 1963, pp. 284–364; R. Donner, *The Regulation of Nationality in International Law* (2nd ed., Irvington-on-Hudson, Transnational Publishers, 1994); I. Ziemele and G. Schram, *l.c.* (note 34), pp. 297–323.

[36] League of Nations, Convention on Certain Questions relating to the Conflict of Nationality Laws, adopted on 12 April 1930, entered into force 1 July 1937, http://www.austlii.edu.au/au/other/dfat/treaties/1938/4.html.

domestic legislation takes. In the context of considerable migration and the lack of harmonisation of domestic nationality laws, it happens that a child does not have the nationality of the State where he/she is born and/or resides. The Human Rights Committee has emphasized that a State is required to adopt every appropriate measure to ensure that a child has a nationality when he/she is born.[37] It does not mean that a State is obliged to grant nationality to every child born in its territory, but the provision should be applied in a manner that ensures that a child is not given less protection because of his/her statelessness.[38]

25. Procedures for the acquisition of nationality differ from State to State and may be rather lengthy. As pointed out, some guarantee against these lengthy procedures may derive from paragraph 2 of Article 24 of the CCPR, requiring that a State, at least, should register a child 'immediately after birth'.[39] This does not guarantee nationality to a child but it ensures some recognition by the legal system concerned. A further guarantee rests on the non-discrimination rule that will be dealt with separately in Chapter Two, 2.3 below.

26. At the same time, the implementation of the rights of children clearly requires the adoption of special measures, as stressed by the Human Rights Committee, and as determined in Article 3 of the CRC. It does not appear that States have objected to this obligation either in the framework of the CCPR, CRC, or other instruments listed at the outset. As for the CCPR, so far only Liechtenstein has made a reservation in relation to Article 24 saying that the granting of nationality will follow the established domestic procedures. As explained, Article 24 does not prohibit the application of domestic procedures in deciding on nationality as long as they comply with the above outlined principles regarding registration and non-discrimination.

27. The ECN, as a regional instrument, sets forth more detailed rules concerning nationality of children. Article 6 provides that each State Party is bound to recognise the right of a child of one of its nationals to an automatic acquisition of nationality. The Article requires that nationality is granted *ex lege* or upon the application, if children, who are born on the territory of a State, are otherwise stateless. As far as the domestic procedures

---

[37] Human Rights Committee, *o.c.* (note 23), para. 8.
[38] *Ibid.*, para. 25.
[39] See M. Nowak, *U.N. Covenant on Civil and Political Rights. CCPR Commentary* (Kehl/Strasbourg/Arlington, N. P. Engel Publishers, 1993), p. 434.

are concerned, the ECN goes further and requires that a possible requirement in national law of lawful and habitual residence for the purposes of
a decision on nationality should not exceed five years.[40]

28. In another regional setting, the Inter-American Court of Human Rights
in its Advisory Opinion of 1984 on the Amendments to the Naturalisation
Provisions of the Constitution of Costa Rica explained that the right to a
nationality is an inherent human right recognised in international law. The
Court went further and explained that international law imposes certain
limits on the broad powers enjoyed by the State relating to nationality.
These powers are circumscribed by the obligation to ensure the full protection of human rights.[41] The Court had to treat proposed amendments to
naturalisation requirements in Costa Rica. It found that, in principle, a State
may from time to time change its naturalisation procedure. However, these
changes should comply with international law. The Court endorsed the
approach adopted by the International Court of Justice in the Nottebohm
case by stating that, even if it is a matter of State discretion to determine
which elements constitute a genuine link between an individual wishing to
naturalize and the State, other States may refuse to recognize nationality
conferred in violation of relevant international law.[42] In the case of Costa
Rica, the Court could not find any potential infringement upon Article 20
since no Costa Rican national would be deprived of nationality, nor would
these amendments prevent a person from acquiring nationality if he/she
wished so. However, the Court pointed out that the amended naturalisation procedure may create a temporary statelessness which is inconsistent
with Article 3 of the Convention on the Nationality of Married Women and
Article 9 of the Convention on the Elimination of All Forms of Discrimination
Against Women.[43]

29. It is true that the recognition of the right to a nationality, even if limited and imperfect, may imply that there should no longer be any stateless
persons. Furthermore, the 1954 Convention on the Status of Stateless Persons

---

[40] Council of Europe, *European Convention on Nationality. Explanatory Report* (Council of Europe
Doc. ETS No. 166, 1997), paras. 49–50. The ECN entered into force in 2000.
[41] Inter-American Court of Human Rights, 'Amendments to the Naturalisation Provisions
of the Constitution of Costa Rica, Advisory Opinion (1984)', *Human Rights Law Journal*, No. 5,
p. 167.
[42] International Court of Justice, *Nottebohm Case*, Second Phase, 1955, I.C.J. Reports 4.
[43] S. Davidson, *The Inter-American Court of Human Rights* (Brookfield, Dartmouth, 1992), pp.
159–161.

and the 1961 Convention on the Reduction of Statelessness[44] spell out, in a rather detailed manner, those principles and rules which the States Parties are required to apply when determining nationality in order to reduce statelessness. The essential provisions of the 1961 Convention for the purposes of the protection of children are as follows. A State Party shall grant its nationality to a person born in its territory who would otherwise be stateless. It may, however, make the granting of this nationality subject to certain conditions. A child born in wedlock in the territory of a State Party, whose mother has the nationality of that State, shall acquire at birth that nationality if it otherwise would be stateless. A foundling found in the territory of a State Party shall, in the absence of proof to the contrary, be considered to have been born within that territory, of parents possessing the nationality of the State. Subject to certain conditions, a State Party shall grant its nationality to a person not born in its territory who would otherwise be stateless, if the nationality of one of his/her parents at the time of the person's birth was that of the State.

30. The ECN likewise provides that domestic laws in matters of nationality shall avoid statelessness. Under the ECN, this applies both to existing nationality laws and new laws which could be adopted in consequence of State succession. It is not always easy, however, to determine to which nationality the individual is entitled. The right to a nationality is not always or necessarily accompanied by corollary obligations of States. Situations of statelessness are not rare, even though there have been persistent attempts to remedy the problem in relation to special groups such as children, or in special circumstances such as State succession.

31. The existing treaty and/or customary rules and principles in relation to statelessness could be summarized as follows. The reduction of statelessness, first of all, is a generally recognized principle with a clear human rights character.[45] The loss of nationality which is not conditioned upon the acquisition of another nationality is not accepted today as being in compliance with the principle of the reduction of statelessness and with other rules

---

[44] United Nations, Convention on the Reduction of Statelessness, adopted on 30 August 1961, entered into force on 13 December 1975, http://www.ohchr.org/english/law/statelessness.htm.

[45] See V. Mikulka, *Second Report on State Succession and its Impact on the Nationality of Natural and Legal Persons* (UN Doc. A/CN.4/474, 1996), p. 11; International Law Commission, *Report of the International Law Commission on the work of its forty-ninth session 12 May–18 July* (UN GA Official Records, 52nd Session, Supp. No. 10 (A/52/10), 1997), pp. 34–35.

and principles of human rights law.[46] The generation of mass statelessness on discriminatory grounds, including political motives, would not be accepted.[47] In situations of State succession, according to the ILC and the Council of Europe, nationals of the predecessor State could not become stateless because they clearly have the right to, at least, one nationality.[48] The ILC considers that the reduction of statelessness is a fundamental premise in dealing with the nationality question in situations of State succession.[49] The recognition that children should acquire a nationality in accordance with the kind of *jus soli* principle, if they are otherwise stateless, is a rule that binds States Parties to the treaties mentioned above. In situations of State succession, the rule is part of customary international law and thus binds all States, old and new. One could even argue that in relation to children there is an *erga omnes* obligation,[50] owed to the international community as such, not to render them stateless in the territory that they are born and/or reside, or are found in.

2.3 *Non-Discrimination Rule*

32. The Human Rights Committee has emphasized that:

> '[N]o discrimination with regard to the acquisition of nationality should be admissible under internal law as between legitimate children and children born out of wedlock or of stateless parents or based on the nationality status of one or both of the parents.'[51] The Human Rights Committee has thus identified grounds, such as the statelessness of the parents, their nationality or marital status, which may not serve to justify distinctions, exclusions, etc., in relation to children.[52]

In addition, it is submitted that the traditional grounds for prohibiting discrimination (that is race, colour, sex, language, religion, national or social

---

[46] H. Batiffol and P. Lagarde, *Droit international privé* (7ième ed., Paris, Librairie générale de droit et de jurisprudence, 1983), vol. 1, pp. 82–83.

[47] R. Hofmann, 'Denationalization and Forced Exile', in: R. Bernhardt (ed.), *Encyclopaedia of Public International Law* (Amsterdam, Elsevier, 1985) vol. 8, pp. 128–133.

[48] See V. Mikulka, *Second Report on State Succession and its Impact on the Nationality of Natural and Legal Persons, o.c.* (note 45), p. 37.

[49] See *ibid.*, p. 11; V. Mikulka, *Third Report on Nationality in Relation to the Succession of States* (UN Doc. A/CN.4/480, 1997), pp. 40–45.

[50] International Court of Justice, *Barcelona Traction, Light and Power Co. case*, 1970, I.C.J. Reports 3.

[51] Human Rights Committee, *o.c.* (note 23), para. 25.

[52] Human Rights Committee, *Communication No. 930/2000: Australia* (UN Doc. CCPR/C/72/D/930/2000, 2001). *Cf. supra* note 30.

origin, property or birth) will also apply when decisions on acquisition by a child of a nationality is taken.

33. There are two main contexts in which nationality legislation could, directly or indirectly, be linked with the non-discrimination rule. First, the provisions of such legislation could be discriminatory in themselves. They might deprive persons of nationality on discriminatory grounds or prevent persons from acquiring nationality on discriminatory grounds. Second, the lack of nationality may serve as a basis for discrimination. Even if non-nationals, in principle, should enjoy almost all human rights, including social and economic benefits where applicable, the problems may and do arise. The Human Rights Committee in its Comment No. 17 had clearly such difficulties in mind as they may affect children.

34. Article 1(2) of the CERD is explicit to the effect that distinctions, preferences, *etc.*, which are made between 'citizens' and 'non-citizens' do not fall within the scope of racial discrimination.[53] Today it is argued that distinctions between nationals and non-nationals, if they are unreasonable or contrary to international obligations, could nevertheless be discriminatory. In General Recommendation No. 11 On Non-citizens, the CERD Committee affirmed that Article 1(2) 'must not be interpreted to detract in any way

---

[53] This provision also raises the question on the relationship between the terms 'citizen' and 'national', as they often appear in international texts. Article 1(3) of the CERD speaks about both citizenship and nationality, while Article 5 provides for the right to a nationality. Considering the variety of terms, it seems that the drafters were aware of the differences in domestic laws in relation to different categories of nationals or citizens. The right to a nationality, as provided in the CERD, seems to refer to the right to citizenship, as determined by domestic law. This has been, at least, the approach of the treaty monitoring body, the CERD Committee. See E. Schwelb, 'The International Convention on the Elimination of All Forms of Racial Discrimination', *International and Comparative Law Quarterly*, 15, 1966, pp. 996–1068; N. Lerner, The U.N. Convention on the Elimination of All Forms of Racial Discrimination: A Commentary (Alphen a.d. Rijn, Sijthoff & Noordhoff, 1970), p. 56. This also suggests that the distinction under Article 1 refers to the distinction between citizens and non-citizens where nationals would fall within the latter category (so-called non-citizen nationals) in those States which recognise in their domestic laws both 'citizens' and 'nationals'. This is similar to the way Article 25 of the CCPR would apply in those States where political rights are granted to citizens and are not granted to non-citizen nationals. See A. Eide, 'Citizenship and International Human Rights Law', in: N.A. Butenschon, U. Davis, and M. Hassassian (eds.), *Citizenship and the State in the Middle East* (Syracuse, Syracuse University Press, 2000), pp. 88–122, at p. 103 (mentioning the examples of the US and the United Kingdom). For the discussion of the problems that the distinction in Article 1(2) of the CERD poses, in particular in the area of the rights of non-citizens, see United Nations, *Prevention of discrimination and protection of indigenous peoples and minorities: The rights of non-citizens, Preliminary report of the Special Rapporteur, Mr David Weissbrodt, submitted in accordance with Sub-Commission decision 2000/103* (UN Doc. E/CN.4/Sub.2/2001/20, 2001), paras. 1, 197–199.

[non-citizens] from the rights and freedoms recognised and enunciated in other instruments, especially the [UDHR]'.[54] In General Recommendation No. 30 of 2004 the CERD Committee confirmed that there should not be any discrimination in the enjoyment of rights and freedoms provided in the CERD depending on citizenship status or immigration.[55]

35. Article 1(3) of the CERD puts forth another interesting qualification. It states that:

> 'Nothing in this Convention may be interpreted as affecting in any way the legal provisions of States Parties concerning nationality, citizenship or naturalization, provided that such provisions do not discriminate against any particular nationality.'[56]

36. Initially, the Convention was indeed not meant to apply to domestic law in relation to the granting of nationality or naturalisation, except when they discriminated against a particular nationality.[57] Since the adoption of the CERD, the rule on the prohibition of discrimination has developed further. The view has emerged that the prohibition of discrimination applies fully to nationality legislation, including naturalisation.[58] In Article 5(d)(iii), the CERD itself links the prohibition of discrimination on the grounds of race, colour, or national or ethnic origin with the right to a nationality, thus affirming that the two are related. The view of the Human Rights

---

[54] CERD Committee, *General Recommendation No. 11: Non-Citizens (Article 1)* (UN Doc. HRI/GEN/1/Rev.5, 2001). See also United Nations, *Declaration on the Human Rights of Individuals Who are not Nationals of the Country in which They Live* (UN GA Res. 40/144, 1985).

[55] CERD Committee, *General Recommendation No. 30: Discrimination Against Non Citizens* (UN Doc. Gen. Rec. No. 30, 2004). *Supra*, note 27.

[56] The debate in the Third Committee was divided on a number of questions, including terms, such as citizenship, nationality or national origin. Varying understandings were attributed to the term 'any particular nationality'. The two main meanings were: (1) nationality in its legal sense denoting the membership in a State; and (2) nationality in its ethnic or national origin sense. Practice developed by the treaty monitoring body, the CERD Committee, seems to have accepted the latter view.

[57] See E. Schwelb, *l.c.* (note 53), pp. 1009–1011; N. Lerner, *o.c.* (note 53), p. 43.

[58] In considering periodic State reports, the CERD Committee has begun to evaluate practices in granting the right to acquire a nationality as well as other human rights to aliens from the point of view of the prohibition of discrimination. The Committee takes a broad view on the scope of the prohibition. In its concluding observations on Pakistan, the CERD Committee emphasized that non-discrimination grounds in the Constitution do not fully exhaust the grounds for non-discrimination provided for in the CERD. In the light of Article 5 of the CERD, a State is required to submit information on the rights of various ethnic, racial or linguistic groups, including non-nationals. CERD Committee, *Concluding Observations: Pakistan* (UN Doc. CERD/C/50/Misc.18 or CERD/C/304/Add.25 1997), para. 18.

Committee on the prohibition of discrimination of children on the basis of the legal or social status enjoyed by their parents, is in line with these developments.

37. Another aspect of the non-discrimination rule is the notion of special or positive measures which States in several human rights instruments are required to undertake in order to ensure *de facto* equality of individuals and/or groups and which are not considered as a discrimination. Such measures are, in principle, temporary in character because, once equality is achieved, the continuous application of special measures is likely to put other groups or individuals in a disadvantageous position.[59]

38. For example, States continue to adopt some provisions in their nationality legislation with a view to supporting the re-integration into the body of nationals of individuals belonging to the same 'core nation', *i.e.* an ethnic or linguistic group identified with the State. States continue to use language requirements in law and practice for their naturalisation purposes. It is a question whether all or some of these practices are discriminatory. The ECN as well as Article 15 of the ILC Articles seem to accept that this type of reference to language or origin in attributing nationality is permitted where such measures do not deprive anyone of a particular nationality.[60] The ILC Articles deal specifically with State succession and thus it could be argued that this practice could apply only in those circumstances, although the question of the relationship between law of State succession and human rights law would remain. At the same time, the ECN accepts it as generally applicable, arguing that it is the practice in many States. It is interesting to note that the ECN does not contain language as one of the possible general grounds of discrimination. This means that it accepts a language requirement as part of domestic nationality laws. It could, however,

---

[59] Articles 1(4) and 2(2) of the CERD. It is possible to see situations where there is a need for long-term measures because the group that they benefit, in view of its characteristics, will always remain disadvantaged. On this point, see further K. Myntti, 'The Prevention of Discrimination v. Protection of Minorities – With Particular Reference to "Special Measures"', *Baltic Yearbook of International Law*, vol. 2, 2002, pp. 199–226.

[60] It was admitted in the Explanatory Report to the ECN that the attribution of nationality on the basis of certain criteria fixed by States may result in preferential treatment. The ILC has taken a similar view. See Council of Europe, *o.c.* (note 40), para. 41, available at http://conventions.coe.int/Treaty/en/Reports/Html/177.htm. The Inter-American Court of Human Rights held that, because a State offers the possibility to acquire nationality to persons who were initially aliens, it is that State which is best able to determine conditions for such a conferral. The Court supported its argument by referring to the judgment of the ICJ in Nottebohm. Inter-American Court of Human Rights, 'Amendments to the Naturalization Provisions of the Constitution of Costa Rica, Advisory Opinion', *l.c.* (note 41), p. 168.

be questioned whether preferential treatment is reasonable when it distinguishes between groups on ethnic or linguistic grounds, thus introducing an element of inequality. It has to be admitted that the question of the applicability of equality considerations in granting nationality has only recently been brought up but not resolved in the international law debate.

39. It is even more of a question whether children should be subject to these various requirements, as the case may be, in domestic nationality laws when they, in principle, have the right to acquire a nationality. It would appear that if the requirements of language, *etc.*, make the acquisition of a nationality by a child unnecessarily complicated, it may be contrary to both the prohibition of discrimination and the obligation not to render children stateless.[61]

Having outlined the existing and emerging rules of international law relevant for the understanding and application of Article 7 of the CRC, the provisions of the Article will be examined in detail below.

---

[61] Such position was taken by the CERD in its observations about the naturalization procedure of non-citizens, including children, in Latvia. *Cf. supra* (note 7).

CHAPTER THREE

SCOPE OF ARTICLE 7

1. '[C]hild Shall Be Registered Immediately After Birth'

40. The CRC Committee has emphasized a positive obligation of States Parties to the CRC to make sure that children are registered properly even in situations where the access to, for example, nomadic families or rural areas in the country is very difficult.[62] The registration must be efficient and the negligence of parents or a State cannot be excused. A system where children are registered in accordance with religion in different religious registers, like in Jordan, may create uncertainty as to whether the child is registered.[63] It raises concerns as to the compliance with the minimum requirement of registration of children after birth. In its concluding observations concerning the situation in Paraguay, the CRC Committee emphasized that:

> 'Children's birth registration should be given priority to ensure that every child is recognised as a person and enjoys his/her full rights. The Committee encourages further steps to ensure birth registration of children, including the establishment of mobile registration offices.'[64]

41. The CRC Committee also had the possibility to pronounce on the obligation of States not to discriminate or otherwise violate the identity of persons through the registration procedure. The registration certificates have to accurately protect and preserve the elements of the identity of a child.[65]

---

[62] CRC Committee, *Concluding Observations: Algeria* (UN Doc. CRC/C/15/Add.76, 1997); *Cyprus* (UN Doc. CRC/C/15/Add.59, 1996), para. 17; *Lao Republic* (UN Doc. CRC/C/15/Add.78, 1997), para. 43; Mongolia (UN Doc. CRC/C/15/Add.48, 1996), para. 13; *Nepal* (UN Doc. CRC/C/15/Add.57, 1996), para. 16. See L. Holmstrom (ed.), *Concluding Observations of the UN Committee on the Rights of the Child. Third to Seventeenth Session (1993-1998)* (The Hague/Boston/London, Martinus Nijhoff Publishers, 2000).

[63] CRC Committee, *Concluding Observations: Jordan* (UN Doc. CRC/C/15/Add.21, 1994), paras. 11–12.

[64] CRC Committee, *Concluding Observations: Paraguay* (UN Doc. CRC/C/15/Add.166, 2001), para. 30.

[65] CRC Committee, *Concluding Observations: Paraguay* (UN Doc. CRC/C/15/Add.27, 1994). para. 10.

The CRC Committee takes a very firm position that non-recognition leads to the lack of enjoyment of human rights and that, therefore, remaining problems in this area have to be diligently solved.[66]

42. The CRC Committee has in some instances treated the issues of registration closely with the issue of acquisition of nationality.[67] There is a difference between the language of Article 7 requiring the registration of a child 'immediately' after birth, on the one hand, and taking measures 'to facilitate applications for citizenship, so as to resolve the situation of stateless children'.[68] Several States, when ratifying the CRC, have made reservations as concerns the application of their citizenship laws. Liechtenstein has not accepted an obligation to grant nationality immediately; it is to be granted under certain conditions.[69] There are States that do not agree with the obligation to eliminate statelessness.[70] Whenever such reservations appear, it is to be hoped that even if children remain stateless in some countries for some period of time, this does not impede their recognition as persons in domestic law through a registration procedure. The CRC Committee has emphasised that even if children remain stateless or are illegal residents, they should enjoy all rights under the CRC and the State should simplify the procedures for legalizing their residence.[71] This principle has underlined the CRC Committee's approach in different situations that children may find themselves in (temporary protection, internal displacement, asylum).[72]

43. Statelessness is to be seen as a threat to the enjoyment of the rights in paragraph 1 as often stated by the CRC Committee and other treaty-monitoring bodies discussed previously.[73] This is very much a meaning of paragraph 2 of the Article. Having a status of a stateless person implies however

---

[66] CRC Committee, *Concluding Observations: China* (UN Doc. CRC/C/15/Add.56, 1996), para. 16.

[67] In relation to the report of Kazakhstan, the Committee notes the efforts of the State as concerns the registration of children but notes with concern 'that some children [. . .] do not acquire nationality at birth'. See CRC Committee, *Concluding Observations: Kazakhstan* (UN Doc. CRC/C/15/Add.213, 2003), para. 32.

[68] *Ibid.*, para. 33.

[69] Reservations and declarations are available at http://www.unhchr.ch/html/menu2/6/crc/treaties/declare-crc.htm.

[70] *E.g.* Japan. See L.J. LeBlanc, *The Convention on the Rights of the Child. UN Lawmaking on Human Rights* (London, University of Nebraska Press, 1995), pp. 109–110.

[71] CRC Committee, *Concluding Observations: Estonia* (UN Doc. CRC/C/15/Add.196, 2003), para. 29.

[72] CRC Committee, *Concluding Observations: Cyprus* (UN Doc. CRC/15/Add.205, 2003), para. 53. For the same approach, see CERD Committee, *o.c.* Chapter Two, 2.3 (note 55).

[73] *Ibid.*

the fact that there is a State which has noted the person concerned. The person is recognised by the law, but the particular status should not bring with it discrimination or other difficulties in the enjoyment of the minimum human rights. Illegal residence, however, would render the rights in Article 7 completely non-existent and is thus irreconcilable with the aim and purpose of the Article and the CRC as such. Registration of children who are illegal residents with some kind of status (*e.g.* as temporary or permanent residents or some other recognition allowing for the exercise of human rights) is therefore the minimum obligation under the CRC so as to provide them with minimum rights within a particular legal system.

44. The drafters have separated the right to registration, name and acquisition of citizenship. As noted by the CRC Committee in its General Comment No. 7, the registration of a child is the minimum guarantee for the enjoyment of his/her rights.[74] This should not be affected by uncertainties as concerns the issue of citizenship or other related status.

2. '[T]he Right From Birth to a Name'

45. The registration means that a child is also given a name for the purposes of his/her identification in the society. In this respect, registration and attribution of name go hand and hand. The requirement of immediacy applies. When the CRC was drafted, the right to a name was never contested, showing certain agreement in this respect.[75] Problems arise in practice concerning the choice of a name. Neither the parents, nor the State is completely free to insist on a name in one form or another. It was explained above under Chapter II.2.1 that the choice of a name should not lead to a discrimination of a particular ethnic, linguistic, *etc.*, group within the State. It should not be such a name that may create hardships to a child in the future.

3. '[T]he Right to Acquire a Nationality'

46. The right of a child to acquire a nationality after birth in Article 7 of the CRC follows the approach adopted by Article 24 of the CCPR. Paragraph 2 of Article 7 recognises that the implementation of this right is subject to

---

[74] The CRC has firmly stated the obligation to register children. See United Nations, *Prevention of discrimination and protection of indigenous peoples and minorities: The rights of non-citizens, Preliminary report of the Special Rapporteur, Mr David Weissbrodt, submitted in accordance with Sub-Commission decision 2000/103, o.c.* (note 53) (UN. Doc. E/CN.4/Sub2/2001/20,2a), paras. 81–82.

[75] L.J. LeBlanc, *o.c.* (note 70), p. 108.

domestic law. Each State can determine the procedures for the acquisition or loss of nationality, albeit within the limits of 'their obligations under the relevant international instruments' and with special attention to situations where the child 'would otherwise be stateless'. This formulation suggests that child statelessness is still a reality, but that national measures in implementing Article 7 of the CRC must seek to eliminate the problem.[76]

47. The CRC Committee has pointed out some specific problems that have generated statelessness of children and that are contrary to the CRC. For example, the Jordanian legislation on nationality has been criticized because it may lead to statelessness since there is no equality between sexes as concerns acquisition of nationality.[77] A similar problem is noted in Lebanon where nationality is not given to a child if the father is a foreigner, while because of the discrimination between sexes nationality of a woman is not passed on.[78] In Libya, children born out of wedlock remain stateless.[79] The human rights standard under the CRC and the other international human rights instruments listed above provide a uniform answer to these instances. Children cannot be deprived of their nationality or the right to acquire nationality and be rendered stateless for reasons of the legal or social status of their parents.

48. Switzerland has made a reservation, similar to Liechtenstein, stating that the granting of a nationality will follow domestic procedures. This indeed puts into question whether Article 7 of the CRC provides for positive obligations as regards the granting of nationality. No country has objected to the Swiss and Liechtenstein reservations. The United Arab Emirates have said that the granting of nationality is a matter of domestic affairs, to which the Netherlands has objected. Article 7 of the CRC allows for the determination of domestic procedures with the aim of implementing the rights

---

[76] Some argue that the CRC Committee in its concluding observations appears less certain of the existing obligation concerning nationality of stateless children. It has stated that children should not suffer in acquiring nationality because one of the parents may not have a nationality. See United Nations, *Prevention of discrimination and protection of indigenous peoples and minorities: The rights of non-citizens, Preliminary report of the Special Rapporteur, Mr David Weissbrodt, submitted in accordance with Sub-Commission decision 2000/103, o.c.* (note 53), paras. 81–82.

[77] CRC Committee, *Concluding Observations: Jordan* (UN Doc. CRC/C/15/Add.21, 1994), para. 11; L. Holmstrom, *o.c.* (note 62), p. 241.

[78] CRC Committee, *Concluding Observations: Lebanon* (UN Doc. CRC/C/15/Add.54, 1996), para 15.

[79] CRC Committee, *Concluding Observations: Libya* (UN Doc. CRC/C/15/Add.84, 1998), para. 18.

under consideration. It also states that to the extent that there are applicable international obligations, domestic procedures have to comply with these obligations. The granting of nationality to children is not a matter that falls exclusively within the domestic affairs of States.

49. Moreover, the CRC enjoys almost universal acceptance. It has, therefore, been suggested that a number of rights pertinent to a child's well being, including the right to acquire a nationality in accordance with the above indicated principles, are recognised as part of customary international law.[80] It has indeed been suggested that the CCPR and the CRC, together with other relevant attempts to avoid statelessness by birth, embody the international rule of *jus soli* where the right of a child to a nationality is concerned, if that child would otherwise become stateless in the country of his/her birth.[81] For example, there was a uniform pressure on the two Baltic States of Estonia and Latvia to amend their citizenship laws in order to allow children born in their territories in families of Soviet time settlers to acquire respective citizenship. The fact that until 1998 it was impossible, was generally viewed as a violation of their international obligations in the field of the rights of children.[82] In view of the CRC Committee, it was a violation of Article 7 of the CRC which confirms that the Article refers to a kind of *jus soli* rule for children and that the procedure for acquisition of nationality without any discrimination has to be clearly spelled out and available to children born in the territory who would otherwise be stateless.

50. An additional guarantee against the abuse of the right of the child to a nationality is the rule that the best interests of a child should be protected, as provided in Article 3 of the CRC. The CRC Committee has noted that some practices in the area of granting nationality are not in the best interests of the child and, as pointed out above, can be discriminatory. For example, the fact that the Myanmar Citizenship Act established three categories of citizenship which opened for the possibility that 'some categories of children and their parents might be stigmatized and/or denied certain rights' raised concerns about the compliance with Articles 2 and 3 of the CRC.[83]

---

[80] J.M.M. Chan, 'The Right to a Nationality as a Human Right: The Current Trend Towards Recognition', *Human Rights Law Journal*, No. 12, 1991, pp. 1–14, at p. 11.

[81] M. Nowak, *o.c.* (note 39), p. 434; J.M.M. Chan, *o.c.* (note 80), p. 11. *Cf. supra* Chapter Two, 2.2.

[82] CRC Committee, *Concluding Observations: Estonia* (UN Doc. CRC/C/15/Add.196, 2003), para. 28.

[83] CRC Committee, *Concluding Observations: Myanmar* (UN Doc. CRC/C/15/Add.69, 1997), para. 14.

4. '[T]he Right to Know and Be Cared for by His or Her Parents'

51. The questions may arise in the framework of adoption procedures where it is common, when a child is adopted, not to disclose the names of the biological parent(s). In other words, the secrecy of adoption still dominates domestic approaches, although experts have come to conclusions that it is most likely not in the best interests of the child.[84]

52. The CRC Committee takes a strong view that the family is the best environment for children and that States are under the obligation to adopt such laws, programmes and policies that strengthen the family.[85] Furthermore, the CRC Committee has objected to laws which do not allow adopted children to find out who their biological parents are.[86] The wording of Article 7 of the CRC is not very explicit in this respect. The adoptive parents could be and normally are parents to the child. Some exchanges between the CRC Committee and States in the framework of the State reports suggest that the CRC Committee takes the view that the term 'parents' in the context of Article 7 and the aims of the CRC includes biological parents and that the child has the right to know, as far as possible, who they are.[87] This right is both part of Article 7 and Article 3 of the CRC since it is considered to be in the best interests of the child to know, as far as possible, the child's birth parents.

---

[84] There is a lot of literature and a lively debate in various related disciplines where the experts favour open adoption. *E.g.* J.E. Nathan, 'Visitation after adoption: In the best interests of the child?', *New York University Law Review*, No. 59, 1984, p. 649; H.D. Grotevant and R.G. McRoy, *Openness in adoption: exploring family connections* (Thousand Oaks, Sage Publications, 1998). Research on this issue was carried out by Kristīne Lemantoviča for the purposes of her Master Thesis entitled 'Is the Secret of Adoption in the Best Interests of the Child' defended at the Riga Graduate School of Law in 2004.

[85] CRC Committee, *Concluding observations: Kazakhstan* (UN Doc. CRC/C/15/Add.213, 2003), para. 41; *Estonia* (UN Doc. CRC/C/15/Add.196, 2003), para. 33.

[86] *E.g.* Czechoslovakia made a declaration to the effect that: 'In cases of irrevocable adoptions [. . .] the non-communication of a natural parent's name or natural parents' names to the child is not in contradiction with this provision'. In subsequent exchanges between the Committee and the Czech Republic it becomes clear that the rule is not stringently applied which confirmed that the Czech Republic could have withdrawn the declaration which was objected to by the Committee as incompatible with Article 7(1). See CRC Committee, *Concluding Observations: Czech Republic* (UN Doc. CRC/C/15/Add.201, 2003), paras. 8–9.

[87] Luxembourg has objected to Article 7 of the CRC in this sense and has submitted a reservation. Also Poland has reservations with respect to Article 7 of the CRC and open adoptions that the Article has come to provide for.

53. In examining the report of Kazakhstan, the Committee noted that 'it is concerned that adoptions are processed in such a way that seriously hinders the right of the child to know, as far as possible, her/his biological parents. [. . .] In light of Articles 3 and 7 of the Convention, the Committee recommends that the State Party undertake all necessary measures to allow all adoptive children to obtain, as far as possible, information on the identity of their parents.'[88]

54. The limitation 'as far as' possible presupposes that there might be circumstances which may limit the right of the child to know the biological parents. In any event, often there will be a need to weigh all the circumstances, but an absolute prohibition on the right to know biological parents is contrary to the CRC.[89]

55. The CRC Committee has also pointed out that it is important to identify the father in the birth certificate even if a child is born to an unmarried couple.[90]

56. As concerns the right to be cared for by one's parents, the most problematic areas concern abandoned children, orphanages and foster care systems, and adoption. In practice, adoption procedures, especially inter-State procedures, can be very cumbersome. Often children spend years in orphanages while lengthy adoption proceedings take place. Situations where a child is placed in temporary care at a young age and the adoption is finally completed nine or ten years later, are an example of extreme cases that are in clear violation of Article 7 of the CRC. In any event, domestic laws and procedures as well as inter-state agreements should design such a system that permits to respect the interest of the child above all to be cared by its parents. The State bears a positive obligation to develop such forms of alternative care that allows for the development of children and respect of their rights.[91] It is true that this implies considerable financial burden on the State.

---

[88] CRC Committee, *Concluding Observations: Kazakhstan* (UN Doc. CRC/C/15/Add.213, 2003, paras. 45–46.

[89] The European Court of Human Rights when weighing interests of the anonymity of the mother who abandoned her child and that of a child to know the name of her mother decided in favour of the rights of the mother. The Court noted that the problem of anonymous birth is a complex one and there is no European consent on the best way to deal with it. The Court noted that the child was 38 when the proceedings took place. See ECtHR, *Odièvre v. France*, 15 January 2003, Judgments and Decisions 2003-III, paras. 44, 47. See also a dissenting opinion by Judge Wildhaber, Bratza, Bonello, Loucaides, Cabral Barreto, Tulkens and Pellompää.

[90] CRC Committee, *Concluding Observations: Ireland* (UN Doc. CRC/C/15/Add.85, 1998), para. 36.

[91] *E.g.* CRC Committee, *Concluding Observations: Kazakhstan* (UN Doc. CRC/C/15/Add.213, 2003, paras. 45–46.

5. '[I]n Accordance with Their National Law...and ...Relevant International Instruments'

57. The second part of Article 7 clearly refers to all rights provided for in part one of the article. This is confirmed by the use of the term 'these rights'. Indeed, registration procedures should take into consideration particular features of a State. More centralized and urbanized States will have different procedures from the States where, for example, a nomadic life-style is still widely present. Whatever the situation is, the national law should provide adequate ways to ensure registration of a child immediately after birth, as required by the CRC. As for the right to name, again national law will reflect the particularities of the language and culture but taking into consideration the limitations imposed by international law. It is true that margin of discretion is considerably wider as concerns the right to a name (*cf. supra* Chapter Three, 2).

58. Some examples have been mentioned of instances when States enter into reservations concerning the application of Article 7 of the CRC saying that it will be applied in accordance with their domestic citizenship laws. Interestingly, unlike similar reservations in relation to other provisions, this has not generated objections as contrary to the object and purpose of the CRC.[92] This can be seen as certain ambivalence that persists among States as far as any regulation of nationality in international law is concerned. It is true however that nationality continues to be determined primarily in accordance with national law. At the same time, there are agreed international standards and States have become Parties to relevant international treaties containing specific rules regarding nationality (see above under Chapter Two, 2.2).

6. '[I]n Particular Where the Child Would Otherwise Be Stateless'

59. It was already established that as concerns children there is an international jus soli rule that requires the attribution of nationality to a child born in the territory of the State concerned if he/she would otherwise be

---

[92] For an overview of all reservations, declarations and objections, see F. Hampson, *Working paper preparatory to the submission of the expanded working paper by Francoise Hampson submitted in accordance with the Sub-Commission decision 2002/17* (UN Doc. E/CN.4/Sub.2/2002/34, 2002).

stateless. This rule would bind States not only because they are Parties to the CRC but also as a matter of customary international law. In this respect, States have been required by the CRC Committee to amend their national laws accordingly and/or take all appropriate measures to reduce the number of stateless children where the problem persists. For example, as concerns the problem of Libyan children born out of wedlock, the CRC Committee emphasized that this is not acceptable from the point of view of the CRC and that the Libyan law has to be reformed.[93] A similar problem was pointed in the Republic of Korea. Not only children born out of wedlock became stateless but also the adoption procedures where a father was not a national were extremely cumbersome.[94] This was contrary to Article 7 of the CRC and the best interests of the child altogether.

---

[93] CRC Committee, *Concluding Observations: Libya* (UN Doc. CRC/C/15/Add.84, 1998), para. 18.

[94] CRC Committee, *Concluding Observations: Republic of Korea* (UN Doc. CRC/C/15/Add.51, 1996), para. 22.

CHAPTER FOUR

CONCLUSIONS

60. Even if the drafters of the CRC did not anticipate problems with the right to registration and the right to a name, State practice shows that different historical and legal traditions have generated problems in this area. While as concerns registration of a child after birth, a State has a very limited margin of discretion, national particularities with regard to names may represent a different situation. It is clear, however, that there should not be any discrimination based on grounds of ethnicity, national origin or language, etc.

61. The right to acquire a nationality now has a fairly precise content in relation to children.[95] However, the right is not always implemented, especially in States which have identified the primary body of nationals on the basis of the jus sanguinis principle. Procedures relating to the acquisition of nationality rely on the length of residence, the age of the applicant and other requirements, but in the process the non-discrimination rule, the prohibition to render children stateless and the prohibition against adopting arbitrary decisions have to be respected. It appears that, if a child would remain stateless for a considerable period of time because of the age requirement or for other reasons, this would violate his/her right to acquire the nationality of the State which has registered the child.

62. Finally, as concerns the right to know his or her parents, the challenge of secrecy of adoptions dominant in domestic practices remains, while the CRC Committee is clearly taking a different approach.

63. Above all, the fundamental principle of the best interests of the child should assist in the interpretation and application of Article 7 of the CRC. In the light of this principle, it is clear that non-registration, statelessness, lack of knowledge of one's roots as part of one's identity and lack of a family environment are not in the best interests of the child.

---

[95] For a detailed analysis of human rights treaties which oblige States to guarantee the right to acquire a nationality for children, if they are otherwise stateless, and for a practical example of an international pressure that could be exercised in this respect, see OSCE High Commissioner on National Minorities, Letter of the OSCE High Commissioner on National Minorities to the Minister for Foreign Affairs of the Republic of Latvia, Valdis Birkavs, of 23 May 1997, *Helsinki Monitor*, No. 9, 1998, pp. 61-63.